Bryn Mawr Greek Commentaries

Epistle of St. Paul to the Romans

Craig Kallendorf

Thomas Library, Bryn Mawr College
Bryn Mawr, Pennsylvania

Copyright ©1991 by **Bryn Mawr Commentaries**

Manufactured in the United States of America
ISBN 0-929524-70-5
Printed and distributed by
Bryn Mawr Commentaries
Thomas Library
Bryn Mawr College
Bryn Mawr, PA 19010

κατὰ ἄνθρωπον λέγω: "I speak according to human standards"; a parenthetical qualification (B-D, 495.3).

3.6 ἐπεί: "for (otherwise)" (B-D, 456.3).

3.7 ἐν τῷ ἐμῷ ψεύσματι: "by my lie" (K).
τί ἔτι κἀγώ (= καὶ ἐγώ): "why then still...I" (B-D, 442.8).

3.8 καὶ μή: "and should we not..."
καθὼς...λέγειν: parenthetical, although the precise syntax of this verse is elusive (B-D, 427.4). The infin. + acc. (ἡμᾶς) is indirect discourse with φασίν.
ὅτι: introduces direct speech and is not to be translated (B-D, 470.1).
ποιήσωμεν: hortatory subjunct.
ἔλθῃ: aor. subjunct. in purpose clause with ἵνα. A sing. verb is especially common with an abstract neut. pl. subject (B-D, 133.3).
ὧν: i.e., τινες.

3.9 προεχόμεθα: "do we excel? are we first?"
οὐ πάντως = πάντως οὐ, "not at all" (B-D, 433.2).
προῃτιασάμεθα: "previously charged," + acc. and infin.

3.10 οὐδέ: "not even"; reinforces οὐ.

3.11 συνίων < συνίημι, "understand."

3.12 ἠχρεώθησαν < ἀχρειόομαι, "be debased."
[οὐκ ἔστιν] ἕως ἑνός: "there is not even one." Brackets enclose material thought intrusive by the editor, here because it is omitted by a group of especially authoritative mss.

3.13 ἀνεῳγμένος < ἀνοίγω, "open."
ἰὸς ἀσπίδων: "poison of snakes."

3.14 ἀρᾶς καὶ πικρίας: "cursing and bitterness"; gen.'s with γέμει.

3.15 ἐκχέαι: aor. infin. explaining ὀξεῖς, "swift to shed."

3.16 σύντριμμα, ταλαιπωρία: "destruction, misery."

3.17 ἔγνωσαν < γινώσκω; gnomic aor. (translate as pres.).

2.25 περιτομή: "circumcision."
ὠφελεῖ ἐὰν νόμον πράσσῃς: a pres. general condition (B-D, 371.4).
ἀκροβυστία: "uncircumcision."

2.26 ἐὰν...φυλάσσῃ...λογισθήσεται: in fut. more vivid condition.
αὐτοῦ: i.e., ὁ ἀκροβυστίαν ἔχων.

2.27 κρινεῖ: liquid fut. < κρίνω.
διά: "while you have"; denotes circumstances (B-D, 223.3).
γράμματος: "Scripture."

2.28 ὁ ἐν τῷ φανερῷ: "outwardly the one (a Jew)."

2.29 περιτομὴ καρδίας: sc. ἐστί.
οὗ: "of whom/which."

3.1 Paul discusses arguments an opponent might bring up. cf. 4.1 ff., 6.1 ff., 6.15 ff., 7.7 ff. (S-H).
τὸ περισσόν: "the advantage."
τοῦ Ἰουδαίου: collective sing. (B-D, 139).

3.2 πολὺ...τρόπον: "much in every way."
ἐπιστεύθησαν: "they (i.e., the Jews) have been entrusted with," + acc.
τὰ λόγια: probably the Mosaic Law and the Messianic promises (S-H).

3.3 τί γάρ: "what difference does it make?"
ἠπίστησαν < ἀπιστέω.
μή: anticipates a negative answer.
καταργήσει < καταργέω, "nullify."

3.4 μὴ γένοιτο: Independent opt. without ἄν = a wish.
γινέσθω = γιγνέσθω = ἔστω (B-D, 98); imper.
ὅπως ἄν δικαιωθῇς...καὶ νικήσεις: purpose clause, with fut. connected by καί added to designate further consequence (B-D, 369.3).
ἐν τῷ κρίνεσθαί σε: "when you are judged"; articular infin., reflecting Hebrew usage (B-D, 404.1).

3.5 συνίστησιν: "proves."
ἐροῦμεν: ἐρῶ is used as fut. of λέγω.

Paul's Letter to the Romans 3

κατ' ἐμέ = ἐμή, a common Hellenistic circumlocution for the possessive and subjective gen. (B-D, 224.1).

1.16 εἰς: "for."
πρῶτον: adv.

1.17 αὐτῷ = τῷ εὐαγγελίῳ.
ἀποκαλύπτεται: "is revealed."
ἐκ πίστεως εἰς πίστιν: "through faith into faith," i.e., "starting from a smaller quantity of faith to produce a larger quantity" (S-H).
καθώς: "as."
ζήσεται < ζάω.

1.18 κατεχόντων: possibly "binding with a spell" rather than the more common "oppressing" (K).

1.19 τὸ γνωστὸν τοῦ θεοῦ: "what can be known about God" (Origen). Paul often uses a neut. sing. adj. like an abstract, generally with a dependent gen. (B-D, 263.2).
ἐν αὐτοῖς: "to them." ἐν is almost superfluous (B-D, 220.1).

1.20 τὰ...ἀόρατα αὐτοῦ: neut. pl. used as abstract (B-D, 263.4).
καθορᾶται: Sing. verb with neut. pl. subject is classical.
εἰς...ἀναπολογήτους: See on 1.11, εἰς...ὑμᾶς.

1.21 γνόντες < γινώσκω.
ἐματαιώθησαν: "they were given to futile speculation."
διαλογισμοῖς: "speculations"; usually in a bad sense in NT (S-H).
καρδία: the broadest term for the human faculties, morally neutral, so that it may house either lustful desires (1.24) or the Spirit (5.5; S-H).

1.22 φάσκοντες: "Since the subject of the principal clause is the same as the subject of the infinitive, it can be omitted. If the infinitive is connected with a predicate adjective, this is made to agree with the subject of the principal clause" (N).
ἐμωράνθησαν < μωραίνω, "make foolish."

1.23 ἤλλαξαν...ἐν: "exchange...for" (< ἀλλάσσω), an unclassical construction (B-D, 179.2).
ἀφθάρτου: "immortal."

2.11 προσωπολημψία: "favoritism," < πρόσωπον + λαμβάνω.

2.12 ἥμαρτον < ἁμαρτάνω, "sin."
ἀπολοῦνται: "will perish"; fut. mid. < ἀπόλλυμι.
ἐν νόμῳ: "under the law." The absence of the article here and in 2.13 is difficult, since Paul normally uses ὁ νόμος for the Mosaic law (B-D, 258.2).
κριθήσονται: "will stand trial," fut. pass. < κρίνω.

2.14 ἔθνη: See on 1.5.
μή: used instead of οὐ with conditional part.'s.
νόμον: obj. of ἔχοντα. The verse plays on the classical contrast between φύσις and νόμος.

2.15 συμμαρτυρούσης...συνειδήσεως: "while their conscience gives evidence in support"; gen. absolute, as is the following expression.
μεταξὺ ἀλλήλων: "on either side."
κατηγορούντων < κατηγορέω, "accuse."

2.17 ἐπονομάζῃ: "call yourself."
ἐπαναπαύῃ: "rely on," + dat.
καυχᾶσαι < καυχάομαι; 2nd sing. pres. indicative.

2.18 τὰ διαφέροντα: "the things making a difference" or "what is best."
κατηχούμενος ἐκ τοῦ νόμου: "instructed by the law."

2.19 πέποιθας: perf. < πείθω; "having confidence that," + acc. and infin.
ὁδηγόν: "guide."

2.20 νηπίων: "children."
μόρφωσιν: "embodiment."

2.21 ὁ οὖν: The construction appears to change here (anacoluthon), since there is no correct apodosis for the protasis in 2.17 ff. (B-D, 467), although verse 21 can be made to qualify as one (S-H).
οὐ: anticipates an affirmative answer, "do you not...?"
κηρύσσων: "preaching," + infin.
μή: used regularly with the imperatival infin.

2.22 βδελυσσόμενος: "abhorring, detesting."
ἱεροσυλεῖς: "rob temples."

1.7. οὖσιν < εἰμί, part.
ἀγαπητοῖς θεοῦ: "beloved by God"; gen. with substantivized verbal adj. designates agent (B-D, 183).
χάρις ὑμῖν καὶ εἰρήνη: combines common Greek (χαίρειν) and Hebrew (Shalom) greetings with the theological meanings of the words (S-H; but cf. K).

1.8 εὐχαριστῶ: "give thanks," + dat.

1.9 λατρεύω: "serve," + dat.
ὡς: "how."
ἀδιαλείπτως: "constantly."
μνείαν: "mention."

1.10 δεόμενος < δέομαι, "ask, pray."
εἴ πως: "if by any means."
ἤδη ποτέ: "some day at last" (K).
εὐοδωθήσομαι < εὐοδόω, "be successful.".
ἐν τῷ θελήματι: ἐν + dat. here = "by."
ἐλθεῖν < ἔρχομαι. The use of complementary infin.'s has been expanded in NT, partly under Hebrew influences (B-D, 392.3).

1.11 ἐπιποθῶ: "desire," + infin.
ἰδεῖν < ὁράω.
μεταδῶ < μεταδίδωμι, "share"; aor. subjunct. in purpose clause.
εἰς τὸ στηριχθῆναι ὑμᾶς: "in order that you might be strengthened"; articular infin. (< στηρίζω) with εἰς to express purpose (B-D, 402.2).

1.12 τοῦτο δέ ἐστιν: "that is," almost a formula in NT.
συμπαρακληθῆναι: "be encouraged together"; infin. expressing purpose.

1.13 θέλω: shortened form of ἐθέλω; followed by subject acc. + infin.
προεθέμην < προτίθημι, "plan," + infin.
καὶ...ἄχρι τοῦ δεῦρο: "and...thus far"; parenthetical, as often with Paul's style (B-D, 465.1).
σχῶ: aor. subjunct. < ἔχω, in purpose clause.

1.14 ὀφειλέτης εἰμί: "I am under obligation," + dat.

1.15 τὸ...πρόθυμον = ἡ προθυμία, "eagerness."

Commentary

Abbreviations:
B-D F. Blass and A. Debrunner, *A Greek Grammar of the New Testament and Other Early Christian Literature*, trans. by R.W. Funk (Chicago 1961)
K E. Käsemann, *Commentary on Romans*, trans. by G.W. Bromiley (Grand Rapids 1980)
M B. Metzger, *A Textual Commentary on the Greek New Testament* (London and New York 1971).
N H.P.V. Nunn, *A Short Syntax of New Testament Greek* (Cambridge 1938^S).
S-H W. Sanday and A.C. Headlam, *A Critical and Exegetical Commentary on The Epistle to the Romans* (New York 1915)
lex. W. Bauer et. al., *A Greek-English Lexicon of the New Testament* (Chicago 1979^2)
sc. "supply"
< "is from" (provides dictionary entry)
NT New Testament
OT Old Testament

1.1 δοῦλος Χριστοῦ Ἰησοῦ: instead of OT δοῦλος Θεοῦ/Κυρίου. The forms are Ἰησοῦς (nom.), Ἰησοῦ (gen. and dat.), Ἰησοῦν (acc.).
ἀφωρισμένος: perf. pass. part. < ἀφορίζω, "set apart, appoint."
εἰς: "for."

1.2 προεπηγγείλατο < προεπαγγέλλομαι, "promise before"; subject = Θεός.

1.3 Δαυίδ: gen. Hebrew names from the Scriptures are often indeclinable.
κατὰ σάρκα: "according to the flesh," i.e., "by earthly descent"; contrasted to κατὰ πνεῦμα in 1.4 (S-H).

1.4 ὁρισθέντος < ὁρίζω, "designate."
Ἰησοῦ Χριστοῦ: in apposition to τοῦ υἱοῦ αὐτοῦ, 1.3.

1.5 ἐλάβομεν < λαμβάνω, "receive"; a literary plu.
εἰς ὑπακοήν: "for obedience," i.e., to cause obedience.
ἔθνεσιν: "Gentiles," i.e., "non-Jews."

1.6 Ἰησοῦ Χριστοῦ: possessive gen.

The text used in preparing this commentary is that of Kurt Aland et al., 3rd corrected ed. (New York: United Bible Societies, 1983). I would like to thank Professors Michael Kumpf and Richard Hamilton for their help with the commentary, and Timothy Moore, Cleve Want, and Luis Costa for their help with the vagaries of word processing in Greek. Finally, I would like to dedicate this volume to Edgar Reinke and John Helms, with whom I began my study of New Testament Greek.

Craig Kallendorf
Texas A&M University
August, 1990

Volume Preface

The Epistle to the Romans was written by the Apostle Paul early in A.D. 58 while he was in Corinth. It is the longest and most systematic of all the epistles, and its carefully reasoned presentation is central to any thoughtful understanding of the Christian heritage. For that reason, Romans is an especially rewarding text to study in the original Greek. The theme of the letter is that mankind is saved through faith. The argument can be organized according to the principles of classical rhetoric--a system which both Paul and his audience in Rome would have known something about--as follows:

I. Introduction (1.1-15)
   A. Salutation (1.1-7)
   B. Paul ingratiates himself to his audience (1.8-15)
II. Proposition: Mankind is saved through faith (1.16-17)
III. Narration of background (1.18-3.20)
   A. Condemnation of the Gentiles (1.18-32)
   B. Condemnation of the Jews (2.1-3.8)
   C. Condemnation of all people (3.9-20)
IV. Proof of the proposition (3.21-5.21)
   A. Statement: All people are saved by faith (3.21-31)
   B. Example: Abraham as a type for the circumcized and the uncircumcized (4.1-25)
   C. Example: Christ compared to Adam (5.1-21)
V. Refutation of objections to the proposition (6.1- 11.36)
   A. Objection: Salvation by faith promotes sin (6.1-8.39)
   A'. Refutation: Comparison of life under sin to life under Christ shows that salvation by faith frees us from sinful living
   B. Objection: Salvation by faith breaks God's promise to Israel (9.1-11.36)
   B'. Refutation: His promises are made to His heirs in faith, to all those who believe that Christ is the fulfillment of the law, to Jew and Gentile alike
VI. Conclusion
   A. Amplification of the proposition through rules of living for those who have faith (12.1-15.13)
      1. Social life within the Christian community (ch. 12)
      2. Political responsibilities (ch. 13)
      3. Tolerance and encouragement for all who act in faith (ch. 14)
      4. Summary (15.1-13)
   B. Paul's missionary plans, with personal greetings (15.14-16.27)

Series Preface

These lexical and grammatical notes are meant not as a full-scale commentary but as a clear and concise aid to the beginning student. The editors have been told to resist their critical impulses and to say only what will help the student read the text. Our commentaries, then, are the beginning of the interpretive process, not the end.

We expect that the student will know the basic Attic declensions and conjugations, basic grammar (the common functions of cases and moods; the common types of clauses and conditions), and how to use a dictionary. In general we have tried to avoid duplication of material easily extractable from the lexicon, but we have included help with the odd verb forms, and recognizing that endless page-flipping can be counter-productive, we have provided the occasional bonus of assistance with uncommon vocabulary.

Richard Hamilton

3.19 φραγῇ < φράσσω, "put to silence"; aor. pass. subjunct. in purpose clause, as is γένηται.
ὑπόδικος: "answerable to," + dat.

3.20 νόμου...ἁμαρτίας: The article is lacking in general assertions (B-D, 258.2). cf. on 2.12.
σάρξ: here, "human being."

3.21 νυνί = νῦν. Intensifying -ι always takes accent.
πεφανέρωται < φανερόω, "make manifest."

3.22 δέ: here introduces an explanation (B-D, 447.8).
διαστολή: "difference."

3.23 ἥμαρτον: See on 2.12.
ὑστεροῦνται: "fall short of," + gen.

3.24 δωρεάν: "as a free gift"; adv.
τῇ...χάριτι: instrumental dat. with δικαιούμενοι.
τῆς ἀπολυτρώσεως: "deliverance, redemption."

3.25 προέθετο < προτίθημι, "display publicly."
ἱλαστήριον: "pity, forgiveness."
εἰς ἔνδειξιν: "for evidence, to give evidence."
διά: "through," here with acc. (K).
πάρεσιν: "remission (of penalty)" (K).
προγεγονότων: perf. part. < προγίνομαι, "happen previously."

3.26 πρὸς τὴν ἔνδειξιν: "to show," expressing purpose (B-D, 239.7).
ἐν τῷ νῦν καιρῷ: "the present time"; νῦν is an adv. functioning like an adj. (B-D, 434).
εἰς τὸ εἶναι αὐτόν: εἰς + acc. of articular infin. expresses purpose (B-D, 402.2).

3.27 ἐξεκλείσθη < ἐκκλείω, "shut out, exclude."
τῶν ἔργων: sc. διά.

3.28 δικαιοῦσθαι...ἄνθρωπον: acc. + infin. with λογιζόμεθα, "pass judgement" (K).

3.29 μόνον: adv.
ναί: "yes indeed."

ἐθνῶν: See on 1.5. In NT, ἔθνη often appears without an article (B-D, 254.3).

3.30 εἴπερ: "seeing as."

4.1 ἐροῦμεν: See on 3.5.
εὑρηκέναι: perf. infin. < εὑρίσκω.
'Αβραάμ: acc.; indeclinable, as is Δαυίδ (4.6). See on 1.3.

4.2 πρὸς θεόν: "with reference to God."

4.3 ἡ γραφή: "Scripture."
ἐλογίσθη αὐτῷ: "it was credited to him," the beginning of a commercial metaphor.

4.4 κατὰ χάριν...κατὰ ὀφείλημα: an antithesis already in Thucydides 2.40.4 (K).

4.5 μή: See on 2.14.
πιστεύοντι...ἐπί: an alternative to πιστεύω + dat., which would be confusing here.
τὸν ἀσεβῆ: "the impious (man)."

4.6 μακαρισμόν: "blessing."

4.7 μακάριοι: "blessed," the highest term a Greek could use to describe a state of felicity; in NT it refers to salvation (K).
ἀφέθησαν: aor. pass. < ἀφίημι, "dismiss, remit."
ἐπεκαλύφθησαν < ἐπικαλύπτω.

4.8 οὐ μή: with aor. subjunct. indicates strong fut. negation; a classical usage, but less emphatic in NT (B-D, 365.3).
λογίσηται: mid.

4.10 ὄντι: modifies τῷ 'Αβραάμ in 4.9.

4.11 ἔλαβεν: See on 1.5.
σφραγῖδα: "seal."

4.12 πατέρα: in parallel with πατέρα, 4.11.
τοῖς οὐκ...μόνον ἀλλὰ καὶ τοῖς: "not only for those...but also for those."
ἴχνεσιν: "footsteps"; dat. with τοῖς στοιχοῦσιν, "those following."

Paul's Letter to the Romans 11

4.13 οὐ...τῷ Ἀβραάμ: sc. ἦν, "Abraham did not have." Dat. of possession emphasizes the obj. of possession (ἡ ἐπαγγελία; B-D, 189.1).
τὸ...κόσμου: The articular infin. (with subject and predicate in acc.) explains ἡ ἐπαγγελία (B-D, 399.1).

4.14 κεκένωται: perf. pass. < κενόω.
κατήργηται: perf. pass. < καταργέω (See on 3.3).

4.15 οὗ: "where."

4.16 ἐκ πίστεως: perhaps = οἱ ἐκ πίστεως κληρονόμοι as in 4.14 or "God's plan rests on faith" (C.K. Barrett, *A Commentary on the Epistle to the Romans* [London 1957]).
ἵνα κατὰ χάριν: sc. ἡ ἐπαγγελία ᾖ.
βεβαίαν: "confirmed."
Ἀβραάμ: gen.

4.17 τέθεικα < τίθημι.
οὗ: The relative, which should be dat. (with ἐπίστευσεν), is assimilated to the case of its referent θεοῦ (dependent on κατέναντι).
τὰ μὴ ὄντα ὡς ὄντα: "the things which do not exist as things existing," i.e., "what does not exist so that it exists" (K).

4.18 παρ' ἐλπίδα ἐπ' ἐλπίδι: "against hope, on the basis of hope."
εἰρημένον: perf. pass. part. < λέγω.

4.19 νενεκρωμένον: perf. pass. part., "made a corpse," i.e., "impotent."
ἑκατονταετής: "a hundred years old"; adj.
που: "approximately" (B-D, 103).
ὑπάρχων = ὤν.
νέκρωσιν: i.e., "barrenness."

4.20 εἰς: "with reference to."
οὐ διεκρίθη: "he did not doubt"; aor. pass. < διακρίνω.
ἐνεδυναμώθη < ἐνδυναμόω, "make strong."
δούς < δίδωμι.

4.21 πληροφορηθείς: "informed, convinced."
ὅ: the unexpressed antecedent is the obj. of ποιῆσαι.

ἐπήγγελται: perf. pass. < ἐπαγγέλλομαι.
δυνατός ἐστιν: sc. θεός.

4.22 ἐλογίσθη: See on 4.3.

4.24 μέλλει: " is about to," + infin.
ἐγείραντα: aor. act. part. < ἐγείρω.

4.25 παρεδόθη: aor. pass. < παραδίδωμι.
παραπτώματα: "sins."

5.2 τὴν προσαγωγήν: "the right to enter."
ἐσχήκαμεν: perf. < ἔχω.
ἐστήκαμεν : "we stand." The perf. (< ἵστημι) has the sense of a pres. (B-D, 341).

5.3 εἰδότες: part. < οἶδα.

5.4 ἡ...ὑπομονὴ δοκιμήν: sc. κατεργάζεται, "endurance (produces) confirmation" (K), as in the next phrase. The verbal ornament in this chapter provides a relief after the dialectical rigor of chapter 4.

5.5 ἐκκέχυται: perf. pass. < ἐκχέω, "pour out."
δοθέντος: aor. pass. < δίδωμι.

5.6 ὄντων ἡμῶν ἀσθενῶν: gen. absolute.
κατὰ καιρόν: "at the right time." The article is often omitted in expressions of time (B-D, 255.3).
ἀπέθανεν: aor. < ἀποθνῄσκω.

5.7 μόλις: "scarcely."
ἀποθανεῖται: fut. < ἀποθνῄσκω.
τάχα...τολμᾷ: for potential opt. (B-D, 385.1), "perhaps...might dare."

5.8 συνίστησιν: "shows."
ὅτι: "in that."
ἔτι ἁμαρτωλῶν ὄντων ἡμῶν: gen. absolute.

5.9 πολλῷ...μᾶλλον: "much more."
σωθησόμεθα: fut. pass. < σῴζω.

5.10 κατηλλάγημεν...καταλλαγέντες: aor. pass. and aor. pass. part. < καταλλάσσω, "reconcile," + dat.

Paul's Letter to the Romans

5.11 **οὐ μόνον δέ:** "not only this."

5.12 **εἰσῆλθεν:** aor. < εἰσέρχομαι.
διῆλθεν < διέρχομαι, "spread."
ἐφ' ᾧ: "for the reason that, because" (B-D, 235.2; K).

5.13 **ἄχρι...νόμου:** "before the law."
ἐλλογεῖται: "is brought into account," as in a ledger (S-H).
μὴ ὄντος νόμου: gen. absolute.

5.14 **Ἀδάμ:** gen., as below; indeclinable.
καί: "even."
ἁμαρτήσαντας: a first aor., often added to an Attic 2nd aor. in koine (B-D, 75).
τοῦ μέλλοντος: "the coming one," i.e., Christ.

5.15 **οὐχ ὡς...οὕτως καί:** a negative comparison.
τοῦ ἑνός: "the one man," i.e., Adam.
ἀπέθανον: See on 5.6.

5.16 **ἁμαρτήσαντος:** The more common and probably correct reading, but some manuscripts have ἁμαρτήματος, which is also attractive given that Paul is playing on nouns in -μα in this passage. This belongs "to the dainties of the Hellenistic artists of style" (B-D, 488.3).

5.19 **παρακοῆς:** "disobedience."
κατεστάθησαν: aor. pass. < καθίστημι, "establish, prove to be."

5.20 **ἵνα πλεονάσῃ:** "in order that...might increase"; aor. subjunct. in purpose clause.
ὑπερεπερίσσευσεν: "increased much more."

6.1 **ἐροῦμεν:** See on 3.5.
ἐπιμένωμεν: deliberative subjunct., used when the subject wonders what to do.

6.2 **μὴ γένοιτο:** See on 3.4.
ἁμαρτίᾳ: dat. of reference, "in regard to."

6.3 **ὅσοι:** "as many as."

6.4 συνετάφημεν: aor. pass. < συνθάπτω, "bury together with," + dat.
ἠγέρθη: aor. pass. < ἐγείρω.

6.5 σύμφυτοι: "united with," + dat. of association (B-D, 194.2).
γεγόναμεν: perf. < γίνομαι.
ἀλλά: "certainly" in apodosis of condition.

6.6 συνεσταυρώθη: aor. pass. < συσταυρόω, "crucify with."
καταργηθῇ: "be done away with."
τοῦ...δουλεύειν ἡμᾶς: See on 1.24.

6.7 δεδικαίωται: here, "freed."

6.8 συζήσομεν < συζάω, "live with," + dat.

6.9 εἰδότες < οἶδα.
αὐτοῦ: dependent on κυριεύει, "rules over."

6.10 ὅ...ἀπέθανεν...ὅ...ζῇ: "The death he died...the life he lived." The substantive must be supplied from context (B-D, 154).
τῇ ἁμαρτίᾳ: See on 6.2.
ἐφάπαξ: "once and for all."

6.11 λογίζεσθε: imper.
ἑαυτούς: In NT and Hellenistic Greek, ἑαυτῶν serves as the reflexive for all three persons (B-D, 64.1).
[εἶναι]: missing in most manuscripts.
Ἰησοῦ: dat. See on 1.1.

6.12 εἰς τὸ ὑπακούειν: See on 3.26, εἰς τὸ εἶναι.

6.13 παριστάνετε: "present"; imper., as μή shows. cf. 6.12.
μέλη < μέλος, "limb."
παραστήσατε: aor. imper. < παρίστημι, "present."
ἑαυτούς: See on 6.11.

6.15 ἁμαρτήσωμεν: deliberative subjunct.

6.16 ᾧ: "to (him) whom"; repeated in ᾧ ὑπακούετε.
ἁμαρτίας: gen. of possession with δοῦλοι, "slaves to sin."

6.17 χάρις...τῷ θεῷ: sc. ἔστω, rarely omitted except in this formula (B-D, 128.6).

Paul's Letter to the Romans 15

ἦτε: imperfect, "were (but no longer are)."
εἰς ὃν παρεδόθητε τύπον: probably τῷ τύπῳ εἰς ὃν παρεδόθητε (< παραδίδωμι) (B-D, 294.5).

6.19 ἀνθρώπινον: adv., "in human terms."
δοῦλα: "(as) slave-things."
εἰς ἁγιασμόν: "for sanctification."

6.21 καρπόν: "advantage, gain."

6.22 αἰώνιον: "eternal," here fem.

6.23 ὀψώνια: "wages."

7.1 γινώσκουσιν: part.
κυριεύει: See on 6.9, αὐτοῦ.

7.2 ὕπανδρος: "married."
δέδεται < δέω, "bind."
κατήργηται ἀπό: "(she) is released from"; perf. indicative < καταργέω.

7.3 ζῶντος τοῦ ἀνδρός: gen. absolute.
μοιχαλίς: "adulteress."
χρηματίσει: "she will be called."
ἀνδρὶ ἑτέρῳ: dat. of possession (B-D, 189.2).
ἀπό: regularly accompanies ἐλευθέρα in NT (B-D, 182.3).
τοῦ μὴ εἶναι...ἑτέρῳ: dependent on ἐλευθέρα or used to show result (see on 1.24).

7.4 εἰς τὸ γενέσθαι ὑμᾶς: See on 3.26, εἰς...αὐτόν.
καρποφορήσωμεν: "bear fruit."

7.5 ἐνηργεῖτο: mid., "were at work."

7.6 κατηργήθημεν ἀπό: See on 7.2.
ἐν ᾧ: sc. τῷ νόμῳ.

7.7 ἐροῦμεν: See on 3.5.
ἔγνων...ᾔδειν < γινώσκω, οἶδα; usually taken as contrary-to-fact. Classical usage would include ἄν in the apodosis (B-D, 360.1).
εἰ μή: "if not, unless, except."
οὐκ ἐπιθυμήσεις: fut. used as imper.

7.8 ἀφορμήν: "opportunity."

7.9 ἐλθούσης (< ἔρχομαι)...τῆς ἐντολῆς: gen. absolute.

7.10 εὑρέθη (< εὑρίσκω): sc. οὖσα, "proved to be..."
αὕτη < οὗτος.

7.13 ἁμαρτία: sc. ἐμοὶ ἐγένετο θάνατος.
φανῇ: aor. pass. subjunct. < φαίνω in purpose clause.
καθ' ὑπερβολήν: "beyond measure."

7.14 οἴδαμεν: Paul uses the plu. for commonly acknowledged truths (cf. 2.2), making this reading preferable to οἶδα μέν (see M).
πεπραμένος ὑπὸ τὴν ἁμαρτίαν: "sold as a slave (< πιπράσκω) under the power of sin," i.e., "being a slave to sin."

7.15 γινώσκω: here, "understand."

7.16 νόμῳ: dat. dependent on σύμφημι, "agree with."
καλός: sc. ὁ νόμος ἐστίν.

7.17 οὐκέτι: probably simply emphatic οὐ.

7.18 τοῦτ' ἔστιν: See on 1.12.
ἀγαθόν: delayed for emphasis.
παράκειται: "is at hand."

7.22 νόμῳ: dat. dependent on συνήδομαι, "joyfully agree with."

7.23 νόμῳ: dat. with ἀντιστρατευόμενον, "being at war with."
νοός: gen. < νοῦς.
αἰχμαλωτίζοντα: "making captive."

7.24 ταλαίπωρος: "wretched."
ῥύσεται: "will release."

7.25 χάρις...τῷ θεῷ: See on 6.17.
νοΐ, σαρκί: instrumental dat.'s.
νόμῳ...νόμῳ: dat. with δουλεύω.

8.1 κατάκριμα: "punishment, doom"; probably not "condemnation." See lex.

Paul's Letter to the Romans

8.3 **τὸ...ἀδύνατον τοῦ νόμου**: "what the law could not do" (B-D, 480.6); in apposition to the whole sentence. The neut. sing. adj. with dependent gen. is a favorite construction of Paul's (B-D, 263.2).
ἐν ᾧ: "because."
διά: here "on account of," in spite of its construction with gen. (K).

8.7 **ὑποτάσσεται**: "is subordinate to," + dat.

8.8 **ἀρέσαι**: aor. infin. < ἀρέσκω, "please," + dat.

8.12 **ὀφειλέται**: "debtors," + gen. of that which one is obligated to do (τοῦ...ζῆν, articular infin.). cf. 1.14.

8.13 **μέλλετε**: + infin. = periphrasis for the fut.

8.15 **υἱοθεσίας**: "adoption."
ἐν ᾧ κράζομεν: "when we cry out."
Αββα: cf. Mk 14.36.

8.16 **πνεύματι**: dat. with συμμαρτυρεῖ, "bears witness with."

8.18 **λογίζομαι**: "I calculate, count up on one side and the other" (S-H).
ἄξια...πρός: "worthy...in comparison with," i.e., "to be compared to" (B-D, 239.8).
ἀποκαλυφθῆναι: aor. pass. infin. < ἀποκαλύπτω, "reveal."

8.19 **ἀποκαραδοκία**: "eager longing."
ἀπεκδέχεται: "await expectantly."

8.20 **ματαιότητι**: "frustration, futility"; dat. dependent on ὑπετάγη, 2nd aor. pass. < ὑποτάσσω.

8.21 **φθορᾶς**: "corruption."

8.22 **συστενάζει καὶ συνωδίνει**: "groans together and suffers great pains together."
τοῦ νῦν: "the present."

8.23 **ἀπαρχήν**: "first portion."
ἐν ἑαυτοῖς: See on 6.11.
ἀπολύτρωσιν: "deliverance."

8.24 τῇ...ἐλπίδι: "in hope"; dat. of manner (S-H).
ἐλπίς: i.e., "the thing hoped for" (S-H).
τίς ἐλπίζει: The καί ("at all, still") found in many manuscripts is acceptable classical usage (B-D, 442.14; cf. M).

8.26 ἀσθενείᾳ: dat. with συναντιλαμβάνεται, "helps."
τό: article substantivizing indirect (deliberative) question that follows (B-D, 267.2).
ὑπερεντυγχάνει: "intercedes."
στεναγμοῖς ἀλαλήτοις: "inexpressible sighings" (K).

8.27 ἐραυνῶν: "examining."
τί: introduces indirect question; sc. ἐστί.
κατὰ θεόν: "according to the will of God." See lex., κατά, 5aα.

8.28 ἀγαπῶσιν: dat. with συνεργεῖ, "work with." (For sing. verb see on 1.20, καθορᾶται.)
κατὰ πρόθεσιν: "according to plan."

8.29 ὅτι: "because, for"; a loose causal connection (lex., 3b).
προέγνω: aor. act. < προγινώσκω, "foreknow, choose beforehand."
προώρισεν: aor. act. < προορίζω, "predestine."
τῆς εἰκόνος: gen. with συμμόρφους, "sharing in the form" (B-D, 182.1).
εἰς τὸ εἶναι αὐτόν: See on 3.26.
πρωτότοκον: "firstborn."

8.32 ἐφείσατο < φείδομαι, "spare," + gen.
χαρίσεται: mid. deponent.

8.34 κατακρινῶν: fut. part., to strengthen the parallel with ἐγκαλέσει (8.33).

8.35 χωρίσει: "will separate."
στενοχωρία: "distress."
μάχαιρα: "sword."

8.36 ὅλην τὴν ἡμέραν: acc. of time, indicating extent.
πρόβατα σφαγῆς: "sheep destined for slaughter" (S-H).

8.38 πέπεισμαι: perf. pass. < πείθω.

Paul's Letter to the Romans

ἐνεστῶτα: "things being present"; perf. part. < ἐνίστημι.

8.39 ὕψωμα: "height(s)."

9.2 ἀδιάλειπτος: "endless."

9.3 ηὐχόμην: "I should wish"; a wish impossible of fulfillment, without ἄν as sometimes in the Attic orators (B-D, 359.2).
ἀνάθεμα: "under the curse of God."
ἀπό: "apart from"; unclassical (B-D, 211).
κατὰ σάρκα: See on 1.3.

9.4 διαθῆκαι: "covenants." God's covenant with Israel was repeatedly renewed (S-H).
νομοθεσία: "giving of the law."

9.5 οἱ πατέρες: "patriarchs."
τὸ κατὰ σάρκα: "insofar as the physical is concerned"; adverbial acc. (B-D, 160). Adding the article strongly emphasizes the limitation (B-D, 266.2). A colon here is desirable to avoid designating ὁ Χριστός as θεός, a practice Paul avoids (see M).
εἰς τοὺς αἰῶνας: See on 1.25.

9.6 Οὐχ οἷον...ὅτι: "It is not so that"; an awkward conflation of οὐχ οἷον and οὐχ ὅτι (B-D, 304).
Ἰσραήλ: gen. of possession; indeclinable, as are the Hebrew names below, 9.7.

9.7 ὅτι: "because."
κληθήσεται: "reckoned, considered" (S-H); fut. pass. < καλέω.

9.8 εἰς: "as."

9.9 ἐλεύσομαι: fut. < ἔρχομαι.

9.10 ἐξ ἑνὸς κοίτην ἔχουσα: "having bed from one man," that is, "having children by one man." This sentence is never finished grammatically (S-H), which in Paul often signals a statement of theological significance (K).
Ἰσαάκ: here, gen.

9.11 μήπω γάρ...πραξάντων: gen. absolute, with the subject the children in 9.9-10, Jacob and Esau.
ἐκλογήν: "election."
πρόθεσις: See on 8.28.

9.12 ἐρρέθη: aor. pass. < λέγω.
μείζων: "greater," i.e., "older"; comp. of μέγας.
ἐλάσσονι: comp. of μικρός.

9.14 μή: See on 3.3.

9.17 ἡ γραφή: See on 4.3.
εἰς αὐτὸ τοῦτο: "for this very reason" (B-D, 290.4).
διαγγελῇ: aor. pass. subjunct.

9.18 σκληρύνει: "makes stubborn."

9.19 ἀνθέστηκεν: perf. with pres. sense (S-H) < ἀνθίστημι, "resist," + dat.

9.20 μενοῦνγε: corrective (B-D, 450.4); "rather, quite the contrary."
ἀνταποκρινόμενος: "answering back."
τὸ πλάσμα: "that which is molded."

9.21 κεραμεύς: "potter."
τοῦ πηλοῦ: "the clay"; gen. with ἔχει ἐξουσίαν, "has a right over," + infin.
φυράματος: "lump."
ὃ μέν...σκεῦος ὃ δέ: "one vessel...another."

9.22 εἰ δέ: "but what if..."
τὸ δυνατὸν αὐτοῦ: "his power." See on 1.19, τὸ γνωστόν.
ἤνεγκεν < φέρω, here "endure."
κατηρτισμένα: perf. pass. part. < καταρτίζω, "fashion, make."
ἀπώλειαν: "destruction."

9.23 καί: "even" or "in fact."
προητοίμασεν: "prepared beforehand."

9.24 οὕς...ἡμᾶς = ἡμᾶς οὕς...

9.25 ἐν τῷ Ὡσηέ: "in the book of Hosea"; indeclinable noun.

τὸν οὐ λαόν μου: i.e., the Gentiles (B-D, 426).
ἠγαπημένην: perf. pass. part. < ἀγαπάω.

9.26 ἔσται: "it will be (that)..."
οὗ: "where."
ἐρρέθη: See on 9.12.

9.27 ἐὰν ᾖ...σωθήσεται: fut. more vivid condition.
ἡ ἄμμος: "the sand."
τὸ ὑπόλειμμα: "the remnant."

9.28 συντέμνων: "cutting short," i.e., "bringing about swiftly."

9.29 προείρηκεν: perf. < προλέγω, "say in advance."
εἰ...ἂν ὡμοιώθημεν: aor. indicatives in condition contrary to fact, past time.
Σόδομα...Γόμορρα: "Sodom...Gomorrah." Both are neut. pls.

9.30 κατέλαβεν: aor. < καταλαμβάνω, "seize," here (metaphorically) "overtake."
δέ: introduces an explanation (B-D, 447.8).

9.31 ἔφθασεν: aor. < φθάνω + εἰς, "win through to" (a racing metaphor; K).

9.32 ὡς: represents the idea subjectively, as a belief of the Jews, rather than as an assertion of Paul's (S-H).
προσέκοψαν < προσκόπτω, "stumble," as προσκόμματος, "stumbling."

9.33 ἰδού: "lo"; probably a particle, not a verb, hence the odd accent.

10.1 μέν: emphasizes subject where speaker reports his state of being (lex., 2). The logical antithesis follows in 10.3 (S-H).
εἰς σωτηρίαν: "for salvation." A number of manuscripts add ἐστίν (see M).

10.2 θεοῦ: objective gen. with ζῆλον, "enthusiasm for God."

10.3 ὑπετάγησαν: See on 8.20.

10.5 δικαιοσύνην: acc. of respect.
αὐτά: probably refers to acts of justice.

10.6 ἀναβήσεται: fut. deponent < ἀναβαίνω.
τοῦτ' ἔστιν: See on 1.12.

10.7 τὴν ἄβυσσον: "the abyss, the underworld." This is the first linking in the NT of Christ's ascension with the descent to Hades (K).

10.8 λέγει: "means"; sc. ἡ γραφή as subject (B-D, 130.3).

10.9 ἐὰν ὁμολογήσῃς...πιστεύσῃς...σωθήσῃ: fut. more vivid condition.
κύριον Ἰησοῦν: sc. ἐστί.
σωθήσῃ: 2nd sing. fut. pass.

10.10 ὁμολογεῖται: "it is confessed," i.e., "one confesses"; impersonal pass. (likewise πιστεύεται), uncommon in NT (B-D, 130.1).

10.12 διαστολή: "distinction."
πλουτῶν εἰς: "being rich toward," i.e., "giving of his wealth generously to."

10.13 ὃς ἂν ἐπικαλέσηται: aor. mid. subjunct. in conditional relative clause.

10.14 ἐπικαλέσωνται: deliberative subjunct. (B-D, 366.1).
οὗ: ἀκούω takes the gen.

10.15 κηρύξωσιν: aor. deliberative subjunct.
ἀποσταλῶσιν: 2nd aor. pass. subjunct. < ἀποστέλλω.
ὡραῖοι: "timely" (K).

10.18 μὴ οὐκ: Since μή suggests a negative answer to a question where the verb is already negated (οὐκ), the expected answer is "yes" (B-D, 427.2). cf. 10.19.
μενοῦνγε: See on 9.20.
ἐξῆλθεν: aor. < ἐξέρχομαι.
πέρατα: "ends."
τῆς οἰκουμένης: "the inhabited (earth)."

10.19 ἔγνω: aor. < γινώσκω.
παραζηλώσω ὑμᾶς ἐπ' οὐκ ἔθνει: "I shall make you jealous of (those who are) not a nation."
ἀσυνέτῳ: "without understanding."

Paul's Letter to the Romans 23

παροργιῶ: fut. παροργίζω, "make angry."

10.20 ἀποτολμᾷ: "is bold."
εὑρέθην: aor. pass. < εὑρίσκω.
[ἐν]: found in some manuscripts to clarify τοῖς...ζητοῦσιν, which, however, is probably related to dat. with words meaning "appear." cf. ἐμφανής, "revealed," + dat., below (B-D, 191.3, 220.1).
ἐγενόμην: aor. < γίνομαι.

10.21 ὅλην τὴν ἡμέραν: "daily"; a semitism (K).
ἐξεπέτασα < ἐκπετάννυμι, "spread out."

11.1 ἀπώσατο: aor. < ἀπωθέομαι, "repudiate."
φυλῆς: "tribe"; gen. of origin (B-D, 162).
Βενιαμίν: "Benjamin," one of the 12 tribes of Israel; indeclinable, here gen.

11.2 προέγνω: See on 8.29.
ἐν Ἠλίᾳ: "in (the story of) Elijah"; a Hebrew usage (B-D, 219.1).
ἐντυγχάνει τῷ θεῷ κατὰ τοῦ Ἰσραήλ: "appeals to (lit., "meets with") God against Israel."

11.3 θυσιαστήρια: "altars."
κατέσκαψαν: "destroyed."
ὑπελείφθην < ὑπολείπω, "leave."

11.4 χρηματισμός: "oracle," i.e., "reply from God."
κατέλιπον: aor. < καταλείπω, "leave behind, reserve, keep."
ἔκαμψαν < κάμπτω, "bend."
τῇ Βάαλ: "Baal," a divinity worshipped by the Semites and opposed by later Hebrew prophets.

11.5 λεῖμμα: "remnant."
γέγονεν: perf. < γίνομαι.

11.6 χάριτι: instrumental dat.
οὐκέτι: sc. ἐστί.

11.7 ἐπέτυχεν: aor. < ἐπιτυγχάνω, "obtain," here + acc.
ἐπωρώθησαν < πωρόω, "petrify, make stubborn."

11.8 ἔδωκεν: aor. < δίδωμι.

κατανύξεως: "numbness."
τοῦ μὴ βλέπειν: See on 1.24.
ὦτα < οὖς.
ἕως τῆς σήμερον ἡμέρας: "until this very day."

11.9 γενηθήτω: 3rd sing. aor. imper. < γίνομαι.
ἡ τράπεζα: "table," here "feast."
εἰς παγίδα...εἰς ἀνταπόδομα: εἰς + acc. with γίνεσθαι.

11.10 σκοτισθήτωσαν: 3rd pl. aor. pass. imper. < σκοτίζω, "make dark."
διὰ παντός: "forever."
σύγκαμψον: 2nd sing. aor. imper. < συγκάμπτω, "(cause to) bend."

11.11 ἔπταισαν < πταίω, "trip, stumble"; whence παραπτώματι, "fall."
αὐτούς: refers to Israel; obj. of παραζηλῶσαι, "make jealous."

11.12 ἥττημα: "failure."
πόσῳ μᾶλλον: "how much more"; dat. of measure.

11.13 ἐφ' ὅσον: "insofar as" (lex., ἐπί, III.3).

11.14 παραζηλώσω...σώσω: aor. subjunct. with εἴ πως (S-H; B-D, 375).
μου τὴν σάρκα: i.e., "my fellow countrymen."

11.15 ἀποβολή: "rejection."
καταλλαγή: "reconciliation."
πρόσλημψις: "acceptance."

11.16 ἀπαρχή: See on 8.23.
φύραμα: See on 9.21.
ῥίζα: "root."

11.17 ἐξεκλάσθησαν: aor. pass. < ἐκκλάω, "break off."
ἀγριέλαιος: "wild olive tree."
ἐνεκεντρίσθης < ἐγκεντρίζω, "stick in, graft."
συγκοινωνός: "sharer in x (gen.) with y (usually dat., here gen.)."
πιότητος < πιότης.

11.18 μὴ κατακαυχῶ: "do not exult over" (2nd sing. pres. imper.) + gen.
βαστάζεις: "lift, support."

11.20 καλῶς: "very well."
ἕστηκας: intransitive perf. < ἵστημι, "stand."
φοβοῦ: pres. imper. < φοβέομαι.

11.21 τῶν...κλάδων...σοῦ: gen.'s with forms of φείδομαι, "spare."
κατὰ φύσιν: "by nature, natural."

11.22 χρηστότητα...ἀποτομίαν...ἀποτομία ... χρηστότης: "mercy...severity (lit., "cutting-off")..." This verbal pattern is called "chiasmus."
πεσόντας: aor. < πίπτω.
ἐπεί: "for (otherwise)" (B-D, 456.3).

11.24 κατὰ φύσιν: opposite of παρὰ φύσιν.
ἐξεκόπης: aor. pass. < ἐκκόπτω.

11.25 ἵνα...ἦτε: pres. subjunct. in purpose clause.
ἑαυτοῖς φρόνιμοι: "wise in your estimation, relying on your own wisdom."
πώρωσις: "stubbornness." cf. 11.7.
ἀπὸ μέρους: "in part."
ἄχρις οὗ: "until (the time) in which."

11.27 αὕτη < οὗτος.
ἀφέλωμαι: aor. mid. subjunct. < ἀφαιρέω, "take away."

11.28 δι' ὑμᾶς: "because of you," i.e., "for your sake."
πατέρας: "ancestors."

11.29 ἀμεταμέλητα: "irrevocable."

11.30 ἠπειθήσατε: aor. < ἀπειθέω, "disobey."
ἠλεήθητε: aor. pass. < ἐλεάω.

11.31 τῷ ὑμετέρῳ ἐλέει: "because (God desired to show) you mercy"; dat. of cause.
ἵνα...ἐλεηθῶσιν: "in order that they might be shown mercy"; aor. pass. subjunct. in purpose clause.

11.32 συνέκλεισεν < συγκλείω, "make a prisoner."

ἵνα...ἐλεήσῃ: aor. subjunct. in purpose clause.

11.33 Ὦ: exclamatory nom.
ἀνεξεραύνητα, ἀνεξιχνίαστοι: "unfathomable, inscrutable."

11.34 σύμβουλος: "adviser."

11.35 προέδωκεν < προδίδωμι, here "give first."
ἀνταποδοθήσεται: fut. pass. < ἀνταποδίδωμι, "repay, return"; here impersonal.

11.36 αὐτῷ ἡ δόξα: "praise (be) to him," a formula based on Jewish liturgy (see lex., δόξα, 3).

12.1 παρακαλῶ: "urge."
διά: "by," idiomatically in urgent statements, perhaps a Latinism = per (B-D, 223.4).
παραστῆσαι: a technical term for presenting a sacrifice.
εὐάρεστον: "pleasing."
τὴν λογικὴν λατρείαν ὑμῶν: "(which is) your spiritual worship"; acc. in apposition to a clause (B-D, 480.6).

12.2 τῷ αἰῶνι τούτῳ: "to this world," dat. with συσχηματίζεσθε, "be conformed to" (or "conform yourself to").
ἀνακαινώσει: "renewal."
ὑμᾶς: subject of infin.
τί τὸ θέλημα τοῦ θεοῦ: indirect question with verb omitted.

12.3 λέγω + infin. = "enjoin, urge," + dat. (παντὶ τῷ ὄντι ἐν ὑμῖν, "every one among you").
δοθείσης: aor. pass. part. < δίδωμι.
ὑπερφρονεῖν...φρονεῖν...φρονεῖν...σωφρονεῖν: Repetition of the same stem is called "paronomasia"; the usage here is quite elegant (B-D, 488.1b).
ἑκάστῳ: with ἐμέρισεν (S-H), "apportioned."

12.4 πρᾶξιν: "function."

12.5 τὸ δέ: "but on the other hand..."
εἷς: "individually."

Paul's Letter to the Romans 27

12.6 διάφορα: "different." To complete the sentence sc. "let us use (them)."
εἴτε...εἴτε: "whether...or...or."
ἀναλογίαν: "proportion."

12.8 ἁπλότητι: "generosity."
προϊστάμενος: pres. part. < προίστημι, "stand before, give aid."
ἱλαρότητι: "cheerfulness."

12.9 ἀνυπόκριτος: sc. ἔστω or ἐστί. The next ten verses are "a very free construction... Participles alternating with adjectives are continuously appended to each other in the exhortation without any posssibility of construing them...It appears as if Paul considered the descriptive participle to be the equivalent of the imperative." (B-D, 468.2).
ἀποστυγοῦντες: "hate/hating."
κολλώμενοι: "be(ing) welded to, hold(ing) on to."

12.10 φιλόστοργοι: "love/loving."
τῇ τιμῇ: dat. of respect.
ἀλλήλους προηγούμενοι: "try to outdo one another," or "esteem one another more highly"; a difficult passage, with two interpretive traditions. See lex., προηγέομαι.

12.11 ὀκνηροί: "slothful."
ζέοντες: "boil(ing)."

12.12 προσκαρτεροῦντες: "be(ing) busily engaged in" (+ dat.).

12.13 κοινωνοῦντες: "share/sharing in" (+ dat.).
φιλοξενίαν: "hospitality."

12.14 καταρᾶσθε: "curse."

12.15 χαίρειν...κλαίειν: imperatival infin's.

12.16 τοῖς ταπεινοῖς συναπαγόμενοι: "accommodate/ accommodating yourself to humble ways" or "associate/ associating with humble folk."
φρόνιμοι παρ' ἑαυτοῖς: See on 11.25.

12.17 προνοούμενοι: "have/having regard for."

12.18 τὸ ἐξ ὑμῶν: "with respect to what is yours" or "for your part"; adverbial acc. (B-D, 160, 266.2).
εἰρηνεύοντες: "live/living in peace."

12.19 δότε: aor. imper. < δίδωμι.
τῇ ὀργῇ: "the wrath (of God)."
ἀνταποδώσω: See on 11.35.

12.20 ἐὰν πεινᾷ...ψώμιζε...ἐὰν διψᾷ, πότιζε: "if he hungers...give him food,...if he thirsts, give him drink."
ἄνθρακας: "burning coals."
σωρεύσεις: "heap up."

12.21 νικῶ: 2nd sing. pres. pass. imper.
ἐν τῷ ἀγαθῷ: ἐν with instrumental dat., in imitation of Hebrew construction (B-D, 219).

13.1 ψυχή: "person," by metonymy from "soul."
ἐξουσίαις ὑπερεχούσαις: "governing authorities."
αἱ...οὖσαι: with ἐξουσία.
τεταγμέναι εἰσίν < τάσσω; common periphrasis for the perf. pass.

13.2 ἀνθέστηκεν: perf. < ἀνθίστημι, "stand against, oppose."
λήψονται: fut. < λαμβάνω.

13.3 φόβος: "that which causes fear" (lex., 1).
ποίει: pres. imper.
ἕξεις: fut. < ἔχω.

13.4 διάκονός ἐστιν: Subject is ἡ ἐξουσία.
ἔκδικος: "agent," representing the one who governs (K).

13.5 ἀνάγκη: sc. ἐστίν.

13.6 φόρους τελεῖτε: "pay taxes."
αὐτὸ τοῦτο: "just this (and nothing else)" (B-D, 290.4).

13.7 ἀπόδοτε: aor. imper. < ἀποδίδωμι.
τῷ...τὸν φόρον: sc. ὀφειλόμενον ἔχοντι, as below. Such free ellipsis is typical of epistolary style (B-D, 481).
τέλος: "tax," as distinct from the tribute paid to a conquering nation (φόρος; S-H).

13.8 τὸν ἕτερον: not with νόμον.

Paul's Letter to the Romans 29

13.9 οὐ μοιχεύσεις...ἀγαπήσεις: The fut. serves as an imper. (B-D, 362).
ἀνακεφαλαιοῦται: "is summed up."

13.10 τῷ πλησίον: "the neighbor"; adv. used as substantive.

13.11 καὶ τοῦτο: "and indeed"; explains what has gone before (B-D, 442.9).
ὥρα: sc. ἐστίν + acc. and infin. (ἐγερθῆναι < ἐγείρω).
ὅτε ἐπιστεύσαμεν: referring to the specific moment when Christianity was accepted (S-H).

13.12 προέκοψεν < προκόπτω, "be far advanced."
ἀποθώμεθα...ἐνδυσώμεθα: "let us put off (< ἀποτίθημι)...let us put on"; hortatory subjunct.'s (aor. mid.).

13.13 εὐσχημόνως: "respectably."
κώμοις καὶ μέθαις...ζήλῳ: "in revelry and drunkenness...jealousy"; dat.'s of manner.
κοίταις: See on 9.10.
ἀσελγείαις: "vices."

13.14 πρόνοιαν: "foresight."

14.1 μὴ εἰς διακρίσεις διαλογισμῶν: "but not for (the purpose of getting into) quarrels about opinions."

14.2 ὃς μὲν...ὁ δέ: "the one...the other." Classical usage prefers ὁ μέν.
φαγεῖν: aor. infin. < ἐσθίω.
λάχανα: "vegetables."

14.3 ἐξουθενείτω: "despise."
προσελάβετο < προσλαμβάνομαι, "welcome."

14.4 τῷ ἰδίῳ κυρίῳ: "before his own master"; dat. of advantage, though rather loosely (B-D, 188.2).
στήκει: "stands"; pres. tense; a Hellenistic formation (B-D, 73).
σταθήσεται: "he will stand firm"; fut. pass. < ἵστημι.
στῆσαι: "make stand, establish"; 1st aor. infin. < ἵστημι.

14.5 [γάρ] = δέ, expressing continuation only, a Pauline usage that may have led to its omission in many manuscripts. See lex., 4, and M.
κρίνει: "prefers...holds in esteem."
ἡμέραν παρ' ἡμέραν: "(one) day in comparison with (another) day." The reference is to observing festive days.
πᾶσαν ἡμέραν: sc. "equally."
πληροφορείσθω: "be fully convinced."

14.6 κυρίῳ: "in honor of the Lord"; dat. of advantage, rather freely (B-D, 188.2).

14.9 εἰς τοῦτο: "for this reason."
ἔζησεν: aor. here of single act.

14.10 τῷ βήματι: "place of judgement."

14.12 λόγον δώσει (< δίδωμι): "will render account"; a legal metaphor (K).

14.13 κρίνωμεν...κρίνατε: "pass judgement...decide."
τὸ μὴ τιθέναι: articular infin., in apposition with τοῦτο (B-D, 399.3).
πρόσκομμα: See on 9.32.
τῷ ἀδελφῷ: dat. of disadvantage.

14.14 πέπεισμαι < πείθω.
κοινόν: "unclean."
εἰ μή = ἀλλά (B-D, 448.8).
τι κοινὸν εἶναι: acc. + infin. with λογιζομένῳ.

14.15 βρῶμα: "food."

14.18 εὐάρεστος: See on 12.1.
δόκιμος: "respected."

14.19 διώκωμεν: probably hortatory subjunct., although many manuscripts record indicative. See M.
οἰκοδομῆς: "house-building, encouragement."

14.20 διὰ προσκόμματος: "with offense (to others)" (B-D, 223.3).

14.21 κρέα: "meat."
μηδὲ ἐν ᾧ: "nor (doing anything else) by which."

14.22 [ἦν] ἔχεις: The omission is colloquial.
ἐν ᾧ δοκιμάζει: "for what he approves."

15.1 δυνατοί: "strong (in faith)."

15.2 τῷ πλησίον: See on 13.10.

15.3 ὀνειδισμοί: "reproaches."
ἐπέπεσαν: aor. < ἐπιπίπτω.

15.4 προεγράφη: aor. pass. < προγράφω.
παρακλήσεως: "comfort."

15.5 δῴη: 2nd aor. independent opt. without ἄν, 3rd sing., a Hellenistic alternative to δοίη (B-D, 95.2). Independent opt. without ἄν indicates an attainable wish (B-D, 384).

15.6 ὁμοθυμαδόν: "with one mind."

15.8 βεβαιῶσαι: "secure, verify."

15.9 τὰ...ἔθνη...δοξάσαι: also dependent on εἰς τό to express purpose. Throughout the passage, ἔθνη should be translated "Gentiles."
ἐξομολογήσομαι: "shall praise," + dat.
ψαλῶ: liquid fut. < ψάλλω, "sing praise."

15.10 εὐφράνθητε: "rejoice"; 2nd pl., aor. pass. imper.

15.12 ἄρχειν: "rule" + gen.; infin. to express purpose.
ἐλπιοῦσιν: fut. < ἐλπίζω; pl. despite neut. subject.

15.13 πληρῶσαι: 3rd sing., aor. opt. (B-D, 85); "fill x (acc.) with y (gen.)."
εἰς τὸ περισσεύειν ὑμᾶς: "so that you might abound."
ἐν δυνάμει: instrumental dat. (B-D, 195).

15.15 τολμηρότερον: "rather boldly"; comp. adv.
ἀπὸ μέρους: "in part," i.e., of this epistle (S-H).
ὡς ἐπαναμιμνῄσκων ὑμᾶς: "with the thought to remind you again." On ὡς + part., see B-D, 425.3.
δοθεῖσαν: See on 12.3.

15.16 ἱερουργοῦντα: "ministering."

ἡ προσφορά: "offering."
εὐπρόσδεκτος: "acceptable."

15.17 τὰ πρὸς τὸν θεόν: "with reference to what concerns God"; adverbial acc. (B-D, 160).

15.18 τι...ὧν: "any of (the things) which."
λόγῳ καὶ ἔργῳ: instrumental dat.'s

15.19 ἀπὸ 'Ιερουσαλὴμ καὶ κύκλῳ: "(beginning) from Jerusalem in an arc" (K).

15.20 ὠνομάσθη: "was named," i.e., "worshipped."
θεμέλιον: "foundation."

15.21 ἀνηγγέλη: aor. pass. < ἀναγγέλλω, "proclaim"; here impersonal.
ὄψονται: fut. < ὁράω.
ἀκηκόασιν: perf. < ἀκούω.
συνήσουσιν: fut. συνίημι, "understand."

15.22 ἐνεκοπτόμην < ἐγκόπτω, "hinder, prevent from," + gen.
τὰ πολλά: "frequently" (K); adverbial acc. (B-D, 160).

15.23 ἐπιποθίαν: "desire."
ἀπό: i.e., "for."

15.24 ὡς ἄν = ὅταν, "whenever," + subjunct. (B-D, 455.1-2).
προπεμφθῆναι: aor. pass. infin. < προπέμπω, "help on the way."
ἐὰν ὑμῶν...ἐμπλησθῶ: "if I have my fill of you(r company)"; ἐμπλησθῶ < ἐμπίμπλημι.
ἀπὸ μέρους: "in part."

15.26 εὐδόκησαν: "considered it good" + infin. For the lack of a temporal augment, see B-D, 67.
κοινωνίαν: "contribution."

15.27 ὀφειλέται...αὐτῶν: "obligated to them."
τοῖς πνευματικοῖς: dat. with ἐκοινώνησαν, "have shared in." For pl. see on 15.12, ἐλπιοῦσιν.
λειτουργῆσαι: "serve," + dat.

15.28 σφραγισάμενος: "having sealed," i.e., "having safely deposited."

Paul's Letter to the Romans 33

ἀπελεύσομαι: fut. < ἀπέρχομαι.
δι' ὑμῶν: i.e., "through your city."

15.30 συναγωνίσασθαι: "fight along with."

15.31 ῥυσθῶ < ῥύομαι, "save, deliver."
εὐπρόσδεκτος: See on 15.16.

15.32 συναναπαύσωμαι: "I rest with."

16.1 συνίστημι: "I recommend."
ἐν Κεγχρεαῖς: Cenchreae was the port for Corinth (S-H).

16.2 καὶ γὰρ αὐτή: "also she herself" (B-D, 277.3).
προστάτις: "helper."

16.4 τράχηλον: "neck."
ὑπέθηκαν: aor. < ὑποτίθημι, "put under, lay down."

16.5 τὴν κατ' οἶκον αὐτῶν ἐκκλησίαν: "the church (meeting) in their private home."

16.6 πολλὰ ἐκοπίασεν: "worked hard"; cognate acc.

16.7 τοὺς συγγενεῖς: i.e., "Jews."
συναιχμαλώτους: "fellow prisoners."
ἐπίσημοι: "outstanding."

16.10 τοὺς ἐκ τῶν Ἀριστοβούλου: "the (Christian brothers) of the (household) of Aristoboulos." An Aristobulus was a grandson of Herod the Great (S-H).

16.11 Ναρκίσσου: possibly the well-known freedman put to death by Agrippina (S-H).

16.13 μητέρα...ἐμοῦ: a strong metaphor, even for Paul.

16.14 Ἑρμᾶν: an abbreviation for several names (Hermagoras, Hermogenes, etc.). Like many of the names in this passage, it is common among slaves and cannot be identified with any specific, known historical figure (S-H).

16.16 ἐν φιλήματι ἁγίῳ: "with a holy kiss."

16.17 διχοστασίας: "divisions."

παρά: "contrary to."
ἐμάθετε: aor. < μανθάνω.
ἐκκλίνετε: "turn aside."

16.18 τῆς χρηστολογίας: "smooth, plausible talk."
εὐλογίας: "flattering speech," rather than the more usual "praise."
ἀκάκων: "innocent, guileless."

16.19 ἀκεραίους: "innocent."

16.20 συντρίψει: "will crush, bruise."

16.22 ὁ γράψας: "who has written down," as distinguished from "composed."

16.23 Γάϊος: possibly the Gaius of 1 Corinthians 1.14. The Christian group probably met in his house (S-H).
ὁ οἰκονόμος τῆς πόλεως: "the city treasurer."

16.24 The earliest and best manuscripts omit this verse, found in the critical apparatus of the United Bible Societies text.

16.25 The doxology has traditionally been printed at the close of chapter 16, but other manuscripts place it at the end of chapter 14 or chapter 15, or at the ends of both chapters 14 and 16. Other manuscripts omit it altogether. See M. According to Origen, Marcion deleted chapters 15 and 16 from his edition.

16.26 ἐπιταγήν: "command."

16.27 εἰς τοὺς αἰῶνας: See on 1.25.